WORLD ABOUT US

ACID RAIN

M. BRIGHT

GLOUCESTER PRESS
London·New York·Toronto·Sydney

© Aladdin Books 1991

Designed and produced by
Aladdin Books Ltd
28 Percy Street
London W1P 9FF

First published in
Great Britain in 1991 by
Franklin Watts Ltd
96 Leonard Street
London EC2A 4RH

Design: David West
Children's
Book Design
Editor: Fiona Robertson
Illustrator: Simon Bishop
Consultant: Brian Gardiner

ISBN 0-7496-0495-6

Printed in Belgium

Contents

Introduction

Rain is something we take very much for granted. All living things, including ourselves, need water to grow healthily. Because rain falls from the sky without seeming to touch anything on the way, we think that it is clean. But in some parts of the world, this rainwater is no longer clean. The smoke and gases which come from factories and cars mix with water in the air to make acid. This acid falls with the rain and is called acid rain.

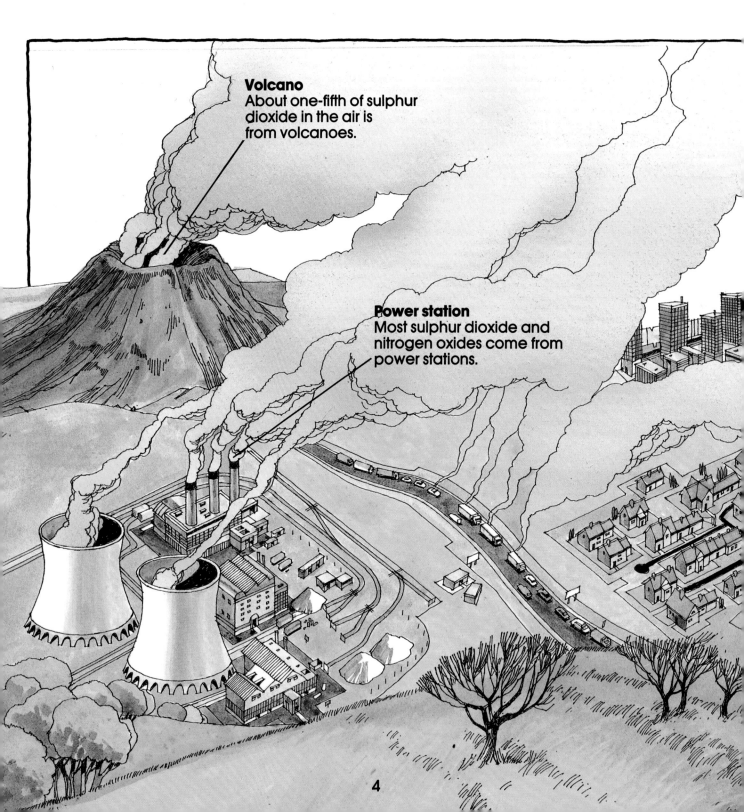

Volcano
About one-fifth of sulphur dioxide in the air is from volcanoes.

Power station
Most sulphur dioxide and nitrogen oxides come from power stations.

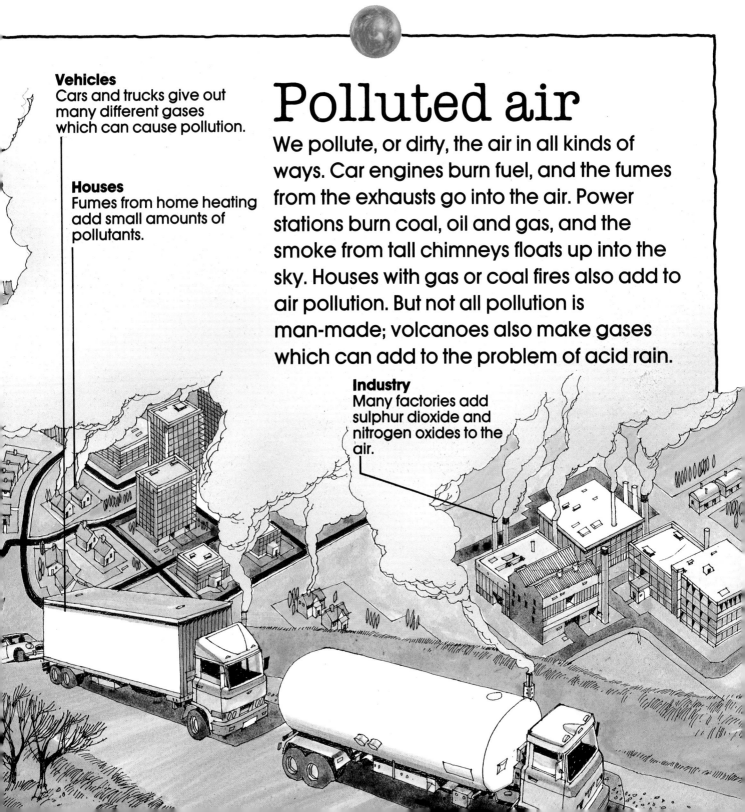

Polluted air

We pollute, or dirty, the air in all kinds of ways. Car engines burn fuel, and the fumes from the exhausts go into the air. Power stations burn coal, oil and gas, and the smoke from tall chimneys floats up into the sky. Houses with gas or coal fires also add to air pollution. But not all pollution is man-made; volcanoes also make gases which can add to the problem of acid rain.

Vehicles
Cars and trucks give out many different gases which can cause pollution.

Houses
Fumes from home heating add small amounts of pollutants.

Industry
Many factories add sulphur dioxide and nitrogen oxides to the air.

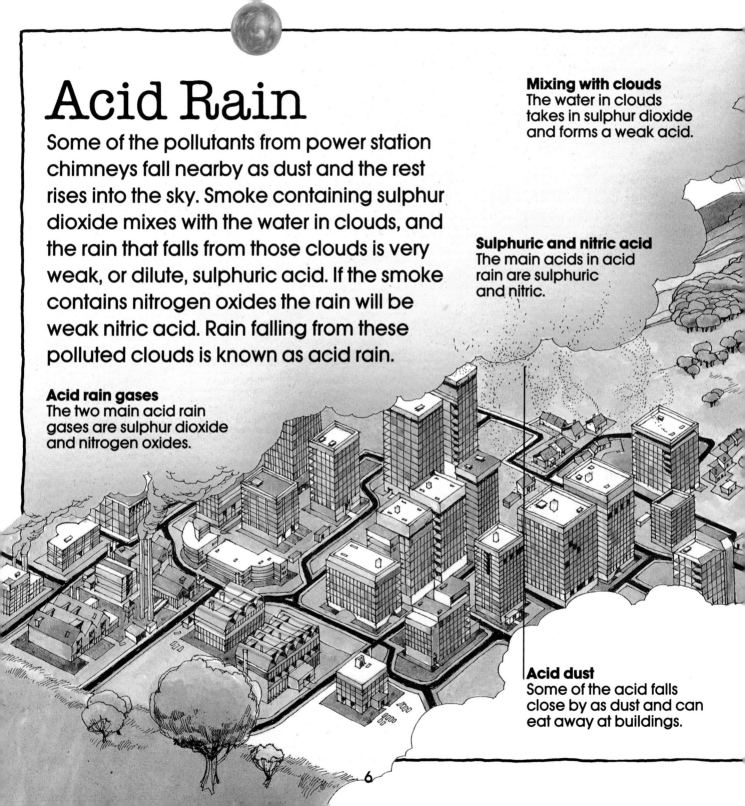

Acid Rain

Some of the pollutants from power station chimneys fall nearby as dust and the rest rises into the sky. Smoke containing sulphur dioxide mixes with the water in clouds, and the rain that falls from those clouds is very weak, or dilute, sulphuric acid. If the smoke contains nitrogen oxides the rain will be weak nitric acid. Rain falling from these polluted clouds is known as acid rain.

Mixing with clouds
The water in clouds takes in sulphur dioxide and forms a weak acid.

Sulphuric and nitric acid
The main acids in acid rain are sulphuric and nitric.

Acid rain gases
The two main acid rain gases are sulphur dioxide and nitrogen oxides.

Acid dust
Some of the acid falls close by as dust and can eat away at buildings.

6

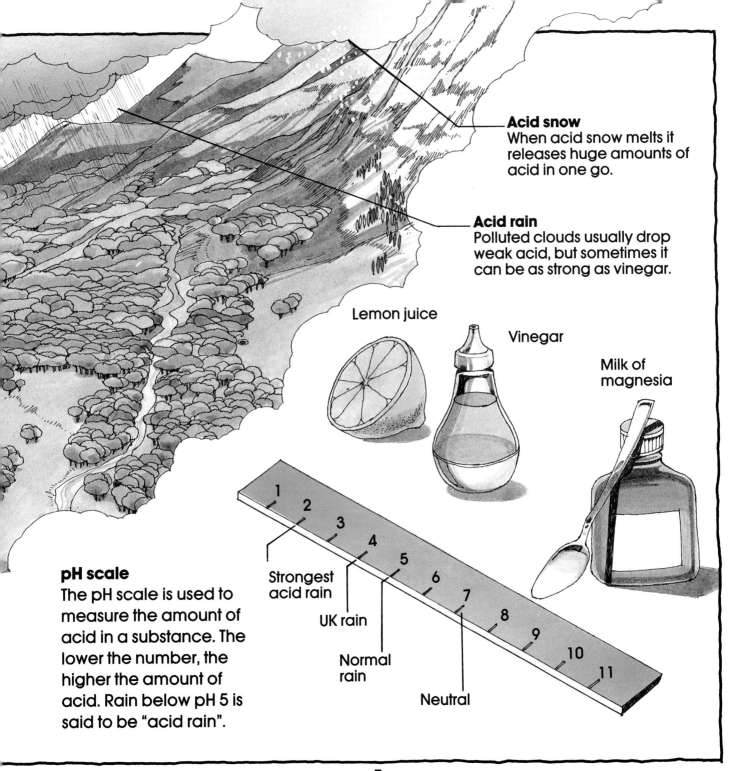

Acid snow
When acid snow melts it releases huge amounts of acid in one go.

Acid rain
Polluted clouds usually drop weak acid, but sometimes it can be as strong as vinegar.

Lemon juice

Vinegar

Milk of magnesia

pH scale
The pH scale is used to measure the amount of acid in a substance. The lower the number, the higher the amount of acid. Rain below pH 5 is said to be "acid rain".

Strongest acid rain

UK rain

Normal rain

Neutral

1 2 3 4 5 6 7 8 9 10 11

Other pollution

The nitrogen oxides that help to produce acid rain also cause other problems, especially in busy towns during the summer. Chemicals called hydrocarbons come mainly from unburnt petrol left over in car exhausts. In sunlight, hydrocarbons mix with nitrogen oxides to make ozone. High up in the sky, ozone protects the Earth from the Sun's harmful rays, but close to the ground it can form a poisonous smog.

Smog caused by pollutants.

Pollutants like lead remain trapped in the atmosphere.

A polluted atmosphere stops fog from clearing.

Sulphur dioxide given out

8

Ozone at low level builds up to form a dangerous smog.

Hydrocarbons come from car exhausts and heating.

9

Spreading Acid Rain

Acid rain is held by the clouds and can be carried up to 500 km each day in whichever direction the wind is blowing. Pollution from one country can therefore travel thousands of kilometres from where it was made and fall in another country. For example, British pollution can be blown across the North Sea to parts of Sweden and Norway in only two or three days.

High chimneys allow smoke to blow further away

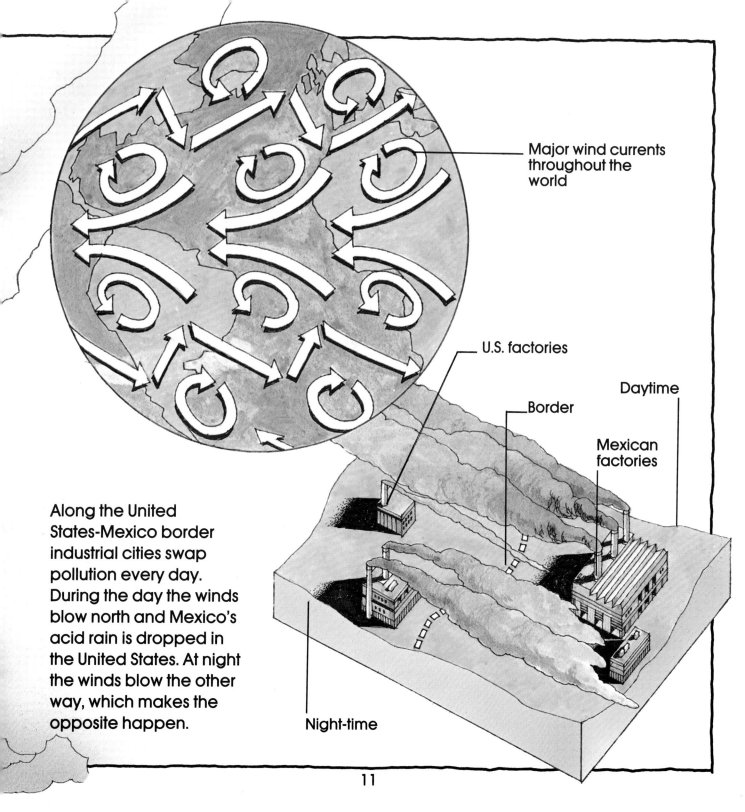

Major wind currents throughout the world

U.S. factories

Border

Daytime

Mexican factories

Along the United States-Mexico border industrial cities swap pollution every day. During the day the winds blow north and Mexico's acid rain is dropped in the United States. At night the winds blow the other way, which makes the opposite happen.

Night-time

11

Who suffers?

Countries like Britain, Germany and Poland have lots of factories and power stations, which give out huge amounts of pollution into the air. This pollution is carried to other countries like Norway and Sweden which have very few factories of their own, but suffer most from the effects of acid rain. In the same way, pollution from American factories led to acid rain falling on Canadian lakes and forests.

Worldwide problems

In developed countries like Britain, the United States and Germany, pollution is now recognised as a major problem. But in many developing countries, like Thailand and India, governments refuse to recognise that pollution is a serious problem. Developing countries are unwilling to stop the growth of factories and industry. As a result, they continue to use more cars and make their cities bigger, which adds to the amount of pollution.

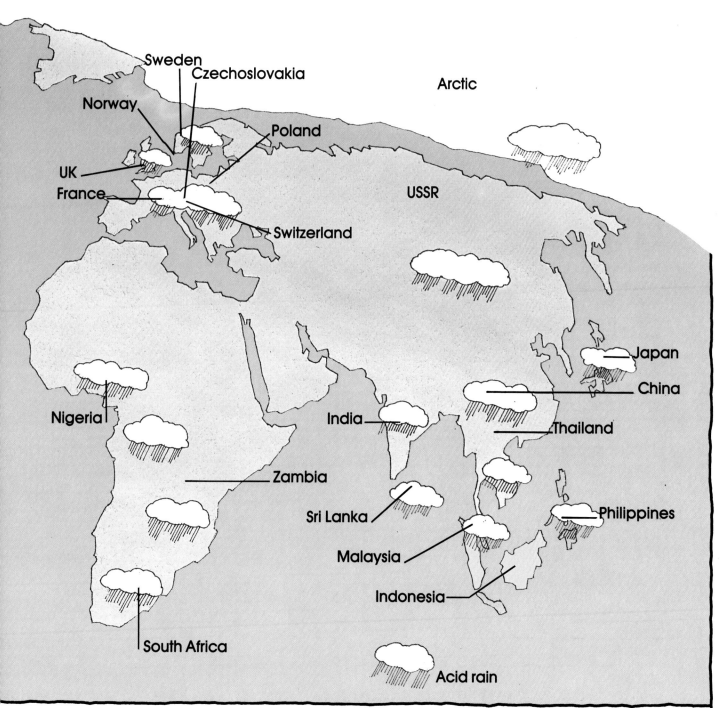

Sweden
Czechoslovakia
Arctic
Norway
Poland
UK
France
Switzerland
USSR
Japan
China
Nigeria
India
Thailand
Zambia
Sri Lanka
Philippines
Malaysia
Indonesia
South Africa
Acid rain

13

The effects

Acid rain can have terrible effects on a forest. The weak acid takes important minerals from the leaves and from the soil. Without these, trees and plants cannot grow properly. They lose their leaves and become very weak. They are then unable to fight against problems such as fungi, diseases or frost, and eventually the whole forest may die.

This forest looks thick and healthy from a distance, but the upper leaves are faded and bleached.

Trees affected by acid rain are weakened and can suffer from attacks by fungi and insects that can kill the tree.

Panic shoots
When trees lose their leaves because of acid rain, they sometimes try to replace them by producing short new buds, known as panic shoots.

Panic shoots

Poisoned soil

Trees and plants need healthy ground to grow in. Acid rain damages soils by destroying many of its vital substances. The food, or nutrients, which a plant needs to grow are washed away by the acid rain, and poisonous metals like aluminium are released from the soil. Also, some pollutants can block the tiny holes on leaves, called stomata. Then the plant cannot take in the air that it needs to survive.

Over 70,000 sq km of forests in 15 European countries have been destroyed by acid rain.

Forests and crops absorb acid water and also poisonous metals released from soil.

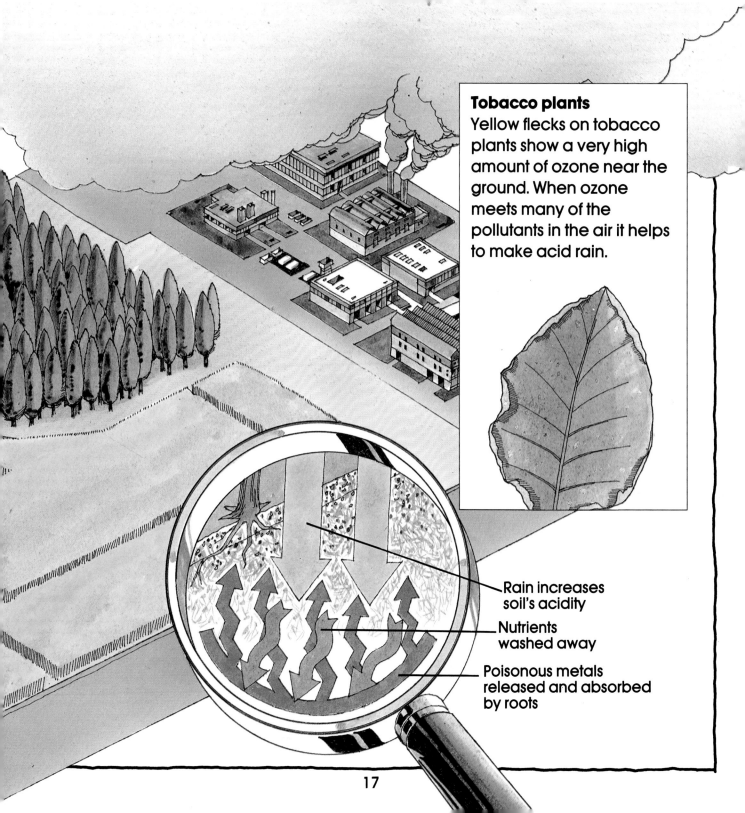

Tobacco plants
Yellow flecks on tobacco plants show a very high amount of ozone near the ground. When ozone meets many of the pollutants in the air it helps to make acid rain.

Rain increases soil's acidity

Nutrients washed away

Poisonous metals released and absorbed by roots

Dead lakes

A lake that has been affected by acid rain looks clean and crystal clear, but contains no life. Many plants and animals cannot survive in acid water. Fish are poisoned by the aluminium which is washed into the lakes. Only water beetles and worms can survive in these conditions.

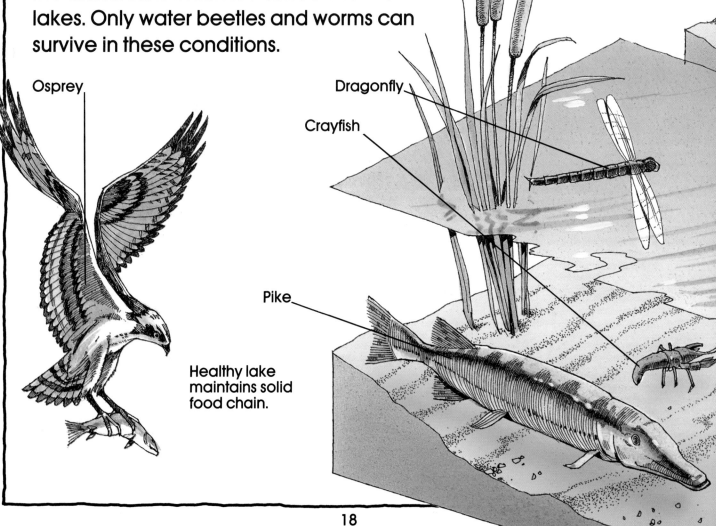

Osprey

Dragonfly

Crayfish

Pike

Healthy lake maintains solid food chain.

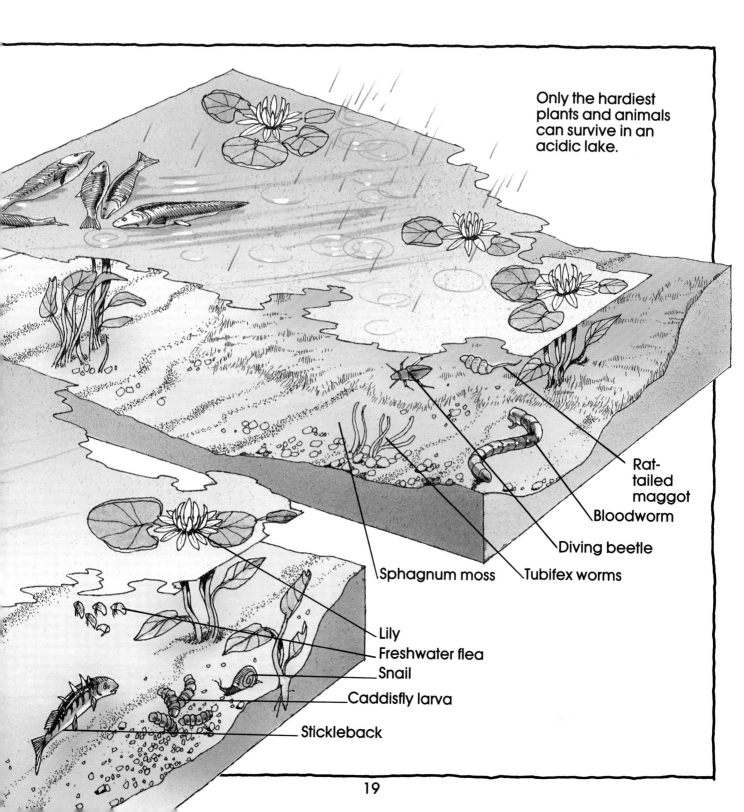

Only the hardiest plants and animals can survive in an acidic lake.

Rat-tailed maggot

Bloodworm

Diving beetle

Sphagnum moss

Tubifex worms

Lily

Freshwater flea

Snail

Caddisfly larva

Stickleback

Crumbling cities

Acid rain not only affects lakes and soils, it can also eat into metal and stone and destroy buildings and statues. In the industrial parts of Poland, local pollution is wearing away railway tracks, and in Greece the Acropolis has suffered more damage in the past 20 years than it did in the last 2,000. In Germany, Cologne Cathedral is falling apart, and in India pollution from an oil refinery threatens the Taj Mahal.

City pollution can affect many buildings and statues nearby.

City buildings and statues become covered with dry acid dust.

Acid reacts with minerals in the stone to make a powdery dust, called gypsum.

Further rain washes away gypsum and stone, destroying the statue.

Every day city life can damage our health. Breathing polluted air can affect the lungs, causing coughing and weakening the body against other illnesses.

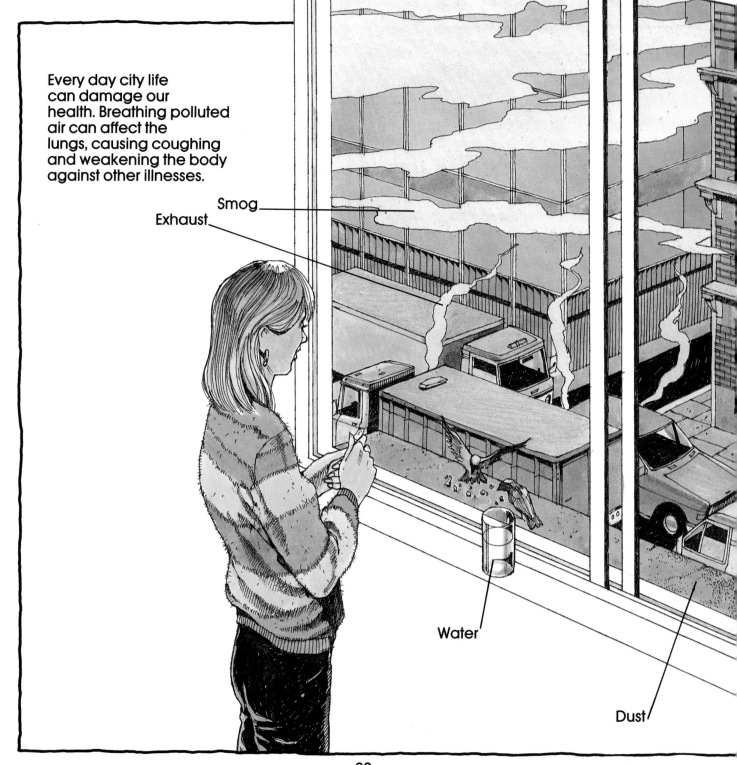

Smog

Exhaust

Water

Dust

Health risks

Pollutants from cars and factories threaten our health too. Car fumes poison the air we breathe. Drinking water is contaminated with chemicals released by acid rain. In parts of Sweden children have diarrhoea and their hair turns green from acid water containing high levels of copper.

Effects on head
Aluminium and lead in water can damage the brain and the nerves. Ozone in cities can make the eyes, nose and throat sore. Carbon monoxide from car fumes causes sleepiness and headaches.

Effects on chest
Many air pollutants, like ozone, can cause asthma and other allergic diseases. The body can easily take in carbon monoxide which stops it from taking in all the oxygen it needs.

Cleaner smoke

If we are willing to spend the money then steps can be taken to control the problem of acid rain. Some types of coal contain less sulphur than others. The gases which come from factory chimneys can be sprayed to remove some of the sulphur dioxide in them. New systems that mix coal with crushed limestone can remove nearly all the sulphur dioxide. By cutting down the pollution which causes acid rain, we can begin to solve the problem.

Gases from factories can be mixed with a chemical that removes nearly all the sulphur from them.

Factories can be fitted with special equipment which reduces the amount of pollutants given off when fuel is burned.

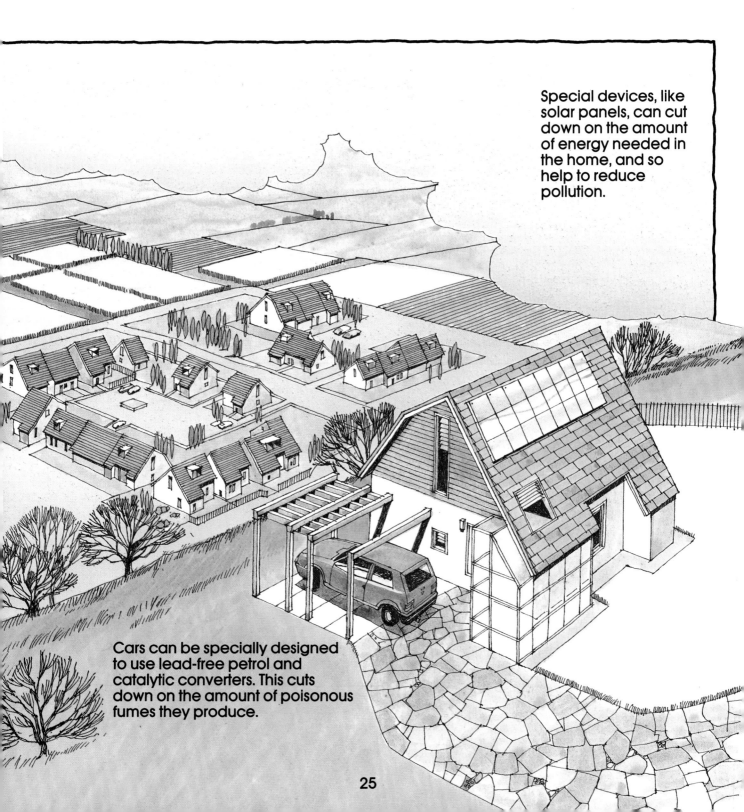

Special devices, like solar panels, can cut down on the amount of energy needed in the home, and so help to reduce pollution.

Cars can be specially designed to use lead-free petrol and catalytic converters. This cuts down on the amount of poisonous fumes they produce.

Taking action

The best way to solve the problem of acid rain is to reduce the amount of pollution. Acid rain is caused by burning coal, oil, petrol and gas. It would be better to change to types of energy which do not cause such pollution, and which last forever, like sun, wind and wave power.

Demos
Conservationists know about the damage caused by acid rain and are trying to get politicians to do something about it.

People from countries all over the world meet to try and reduce the problem of pollution. Their aim is to cut down on the amount of sulphur dioxide produced, and also to try and reduce the use of products containing CFCs.

Liming lakes
Acid lakes can be made fit for life once again by putting lime into them. Lime acts against the effects of the acid rain. But this method only works for a short time and cannot be used for ever.

Rain file

The solution to one problem can often create another problem somewhere else. If more limestone is used in more efficient furnaces then we will need to dig bigger and uglier limestone quarries. Then there is the problem of what to do with the waste lime.

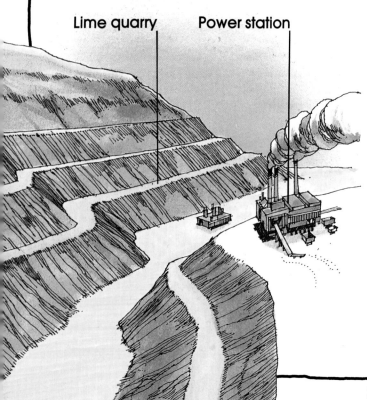

Lime quarry   Power station

Mangrove swamps are home to many different kinds of wildlife. But acid rain can easily destroy many of the plants and animals that live there. Only thick slimes of algae can survive in polluted waters. These slimes use up all the oxygen in the water, which means that fish die. Animals like crocodiles therefore have nothing to eat.

The London smogs were caused by pollutants in the fog around the city. They occurred in the cold, early mornings of December and January. They caused people to suffer from serious lung problems and 4,000 people died in 1952. The Clean Air Act of 1956 stopped the pollution.

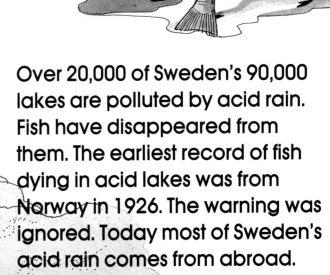

Over 20,000 of Sweden's 90,000 lakes are polluted by acid rain. Fish have disappeared from them. The earliest record of fish dying in acid lakes was from Norway in 1926. The warning was ignored. Today most of Sweden's acid rain comes from abroad.

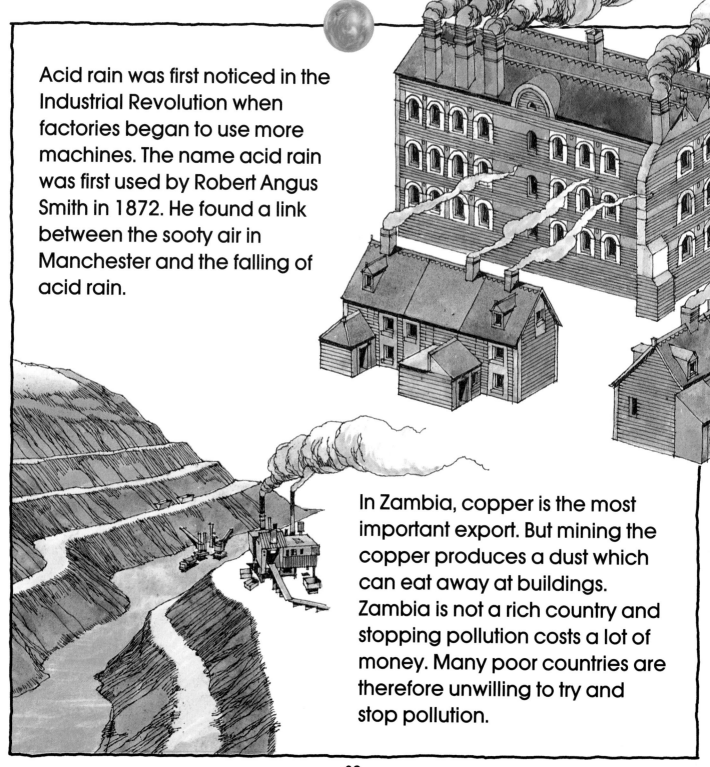

Acid rain was first noticed in the Industrial Revolution when factories began to use more machines. The name acid rain was first used by Robert Angus Smith in 1872. He found a link between the sooty air in Manchester and the falling of acid rain.

In Zambia, copper is the most important export. But mining the copper produces a dust which can eat away at buildings. Zambia is not a rich country and stopping pollution costs a lot of money. Many poor countries are therefore unwilling to try and stop pollution.

Glossary

Acid rain
Water in the air mixes with the pollution which comes from cars, factories and power stations to make acids. These acids then fall to the ground with rain.

Atmosphere
The layer of gases that surrounds the Earth. It is about 700km thick.

Hydrocarbons
These come from car exhausts. When they mix with nitrogen oxides and sunlight in the atmosphere, they form a low-level ozone which can be dangerous.

Oxides of nitrogen
They are made when fuels are burned. They also come from fertilizers used in farming. They help to form acid rain. When they mix with water in the atmosphere, they make acid rain.

Oxides of sulphur
They are made when fossil fuels like coal, oil and gas are burned. When they mix with water in the atmosphere they make sulphuric acid. The most common type of sulphur pollution is caused by sulphur dioxide.

Ozone
A colourless gas which forms the ozone layer in the atmosphere. This layer is vital to life on Earth as it stops harmful UV light from the Sun getting to Earth. But when ozone mixes with hydrocarbons and sunlight at lower levels, it can form a dangerous smog.

Index